Strathearn Environs & Royal Forteviot
Project Report 2006-2009

Contents

Introduction	4
Forteviot and SERF	6
Archaeology of Forteviot	8
The Strathearn Environs	10
Forteviot Prehistoric Complex	12
A Neolithic Arena: Palisaded Enclosure	14
Cremation Cemetery, Timber Circle and Henge Monument	16
Forteviot Cist and Dagger Burial	20
Pictish Forteviot	24
Searching for the Pictish Palace	26
Pictish Cemetery	28
Forts around Forteviot	32
Jackschairs Wood	34
Dunknock	36
Green of Invermay Enclosure and Doocot	38
Early Chapels	42
Exmagirdle	44
Muckersie	46
Dunning	47
Upland Survey	
SERF: Research in Progress	
Timeline	
Acknowledgements	

Introduction

No place has a better claim to be the cradle of Scotland than Strathearn where the Pictish kingdom evolved into the Kingdom of the Scots. Given its agricultural wealth, it is no surprise that the fertile east midlands provided the foundations for the Scottish kingdom, or that it attracted the attention of the earliest prehistoric farming peoples who transformed the landscape into a monumental ceremonial centre. These peoples, separated by over 2000 years, were drawn to the same location at Forteviot. This booklet describes the first phase of the Strathearn Environs and Royal Forteviot (SERF) project; a long-term project designed to explore the complex prehistoric and medieval roots of Scotland.

Understanding the influences of agriculture is one of the key challenges facing the archaeologist. The fertility of the land was responsible for sustaining the nation, but continuous cultivation has also eroded and obscured the physical evidence of the past. However, buried archaeological structures can survive to produce patterns in crops that can be seen from the air, thus pin-pointing ancient sites and guiding archaeological research.

Since 2006, archaeologists from the Universities of Glasgow and Aberdeen, with the help of local volunteers, have been exploring Forteviot and the neighbouring parishes of Dunning and Forgandenny. Excavations at Forteviot have been complemented by excavations of nearby prehistoric hillforts, building surveys of ancient churches and field survey of the unimproved uplands of the Ochils. The overall goal is to investigate the social, political, ideological and environmental developments of Forteviot and its environs from the earliest farming communities from over 5000 years ago to the 19th century. Much work remains to be done, but we have made significant progress in understanding the chronology and development of the archaeological landscape and made some spectacular discoveries along the way.

Another key aim of the SERF project is to make this new knowledge accessible to a wide audience, to encourage active participation by the local community and to build awareness of the importance of Forteviot and Strathearn amongst an international audience. Through the generous support of Perth and Kinross Heritage Trust, this booklet is one way in which we are making our initial findings of this project available to a wider audience.

Clockwise from top left: Excavating at the Late Neolithic henge site; Carefully digging a cremation burial; Recording the Early Bronze Age cist; Giving a tour to local primary school pupils and teachers; Background: taking time to consult maps on the walkover survey of the uplands

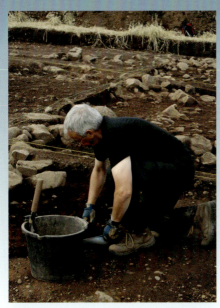

Forteviot and SERF

Forteviot occupies a special place in the history of Scotland. The death of King Kenneth mac Alpin, one of the last kings of the Picts and arguably the first king of Scotland, was recorded at the 'palace' of Forteviot in AD 858. This site was a major royal centre in a fledgling Scottish nation. Forteviot is also the location of one of the most extensive concentrations of prehistoric ritual monuments in mainland Scotland.

It is these two episodes of landscape use, separated in time but physically linked which provide the focus of the SERF project. What is significant about Forteviot and Strathearn that enabled such important regional centres to develop at such different times under such different social and political conditions? The first step in beginning to answer this question is to explore the archaeological evidence of Forteviot and its wider landscape.

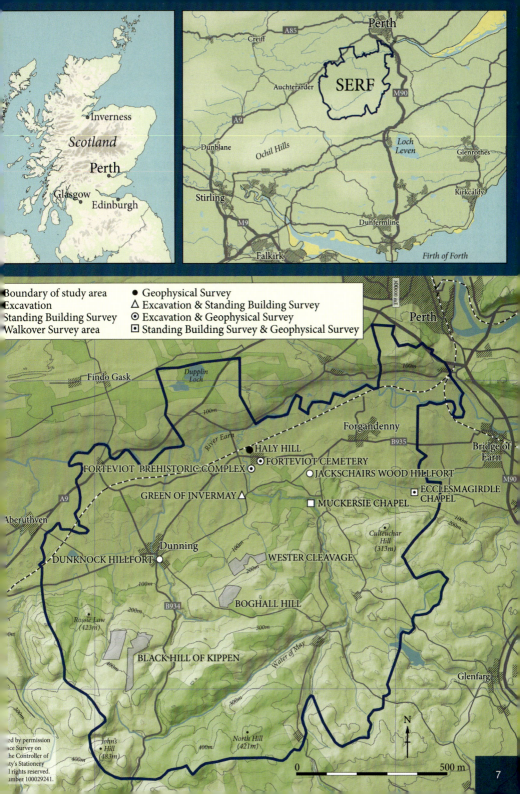

Archaeology of Forteviot

In the fields surrounding the village of Forteviot there is a wide variety of archaeological monuments. Their remains are now largely invisible because the ancient structures were made predominantly of wood and earth. That wood has decayed and the upstanding earthen features have been eroded by centuries of ploughing. Nonetheless, evidence of prehistoric activity survives below ground and has been revealed by aerial photography through patterns in crop growth.

Prehistoric

Across the fields to the south of Forteviot village are the traces of a most remarkable concentration of prehistoric monuments, most of which are thought to be Neolithic in date. These include a large timber enclosure, approximately 250m in diameter, three ritual enclosures known as henges and a range of additional features identified as burial mounds and pits. An extraordinary survivor of this prehistoric monument complex is a large cairn, Mijas, preserved in the pasture just to the west of the cropmarks.

Pictish

Intermingled with the main group of prehistoric monuments and clustered in a separate cemetery to the east of the village are the remains of Pictish barrows and graves which were originally identified from cropmarks. These burials belong to the era when Forteviot was an early medieval power centre and show that the Picts sought to link their burials with those of their ancestors.

Forteviot's royal status is underscored by its exceptional collection of early medieval sculpture, including the unique arch from a church (now in the National Museum of Scotland), fragments of several Pictish crosses and the magnificent Dupplin Cross, now in St Serf's Dunning, but formerly overlooking Forteviot on the lower slopes of the Gask Ridge.

By the 10th century AD there was a shift in the royal power centre from Forteviot to Scone and Dunning, about which almost nothing is known. In the following centuries, farming and agriculture became the dominant activity around Forteviot. Today, the layout and most of the buildings of Forteviot village date from the 1920s when it was rebuilt by Lord Forteviot, based on an Arts and Crafts design by James Miller.

Right: Aerial photograph showing the cropmarks of the Pictish cemetery at Forteviot

The Strathearn Environs

Neither Neolithic nor Pictish Forteviot existed in isolation, therefore understanding the context of the surrounding landscape forms a significant strand of the project. Modern and recent land use has had a varied, and often damaging, effect on the survival and visibility of archaeological remains. Therefore, the condition of past monuments can vary depending on their environmental location. Consequently different methods of archaeological investigation have to be employed. In the cultivated valley bottom, upstanding features of sites have largely been destroyed and only survive as cropmarks visible from the air. In woodland areas and estate policies there are the remains of hillforts and barrows, which can be measured and recorded in more detail, while in the uplands – above the level cultivated today – whole landscapes of settlement, field systems and routeways can survive and need to be identified and teased apart through the survey of more extensive landscapes.

The SERF Study Area

The framework for the SERF landscape study area comes from the ancient parishes which have been in existence for at least 800 years and probably much longer. The antiquity of these divisions provide a meaningful boundary for the study and invite further investigation into the changing organisation of the landscape. The importance of the ancient parish is that it defined the community, so the alteration to the extent and location of the parish reflects changes in society as a whole. The administrative history is also relevant for understanding the emergence of medieval lordship and the creation of landed estates, which have had a huge influence on why Strathearn is the way it is.

The initial idea was to examine the parish of Forteviot flanked by Dunning and Forgandenny, because it forms a coherent block of ground running from the top of the Ochils down to the River Earn. As we looked into the history of the parishes, it became clear that behind the simplified modern boundaries was a complex evolution involving the incorporation of detached areas and lost parishes.

Background image: excerpt from OS First Edition 1:10560 scale map, 1862

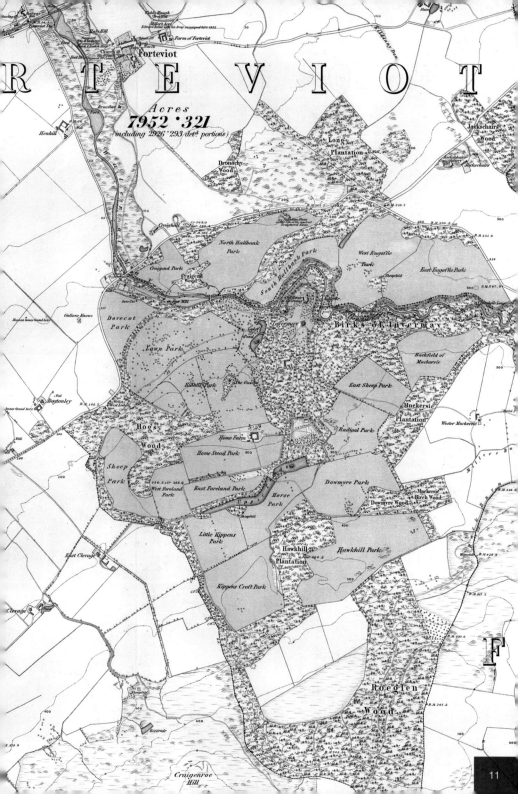

Forteviot Prehistoric Complex

The cropmarks south of Forteviot village present a dense concentration of enclosures and ceremonial structures, which excavation is beginning to help us make sense of. The largest and earliest structure is what would have been a huge arena defined by massive oak posts, thought to have been erected by the early farmers of the Neolithic period. Inside and adjacent to this arena are three or four smaller ritual enclosures, known as henges, as well as a range of other pits. Excavations at the largest of these henges have revealed a surprisingly long and varied history of use and modification of this monument from the Later Neolithic (from 3000 - 2700 BC) to the medieval periods. Importantly, our excavations have revealed much more information than it would have been possible to learn from aerial photographs alone.

Right: An aerial photograph with the cropmarks of the prehistoric monuments outlined in red

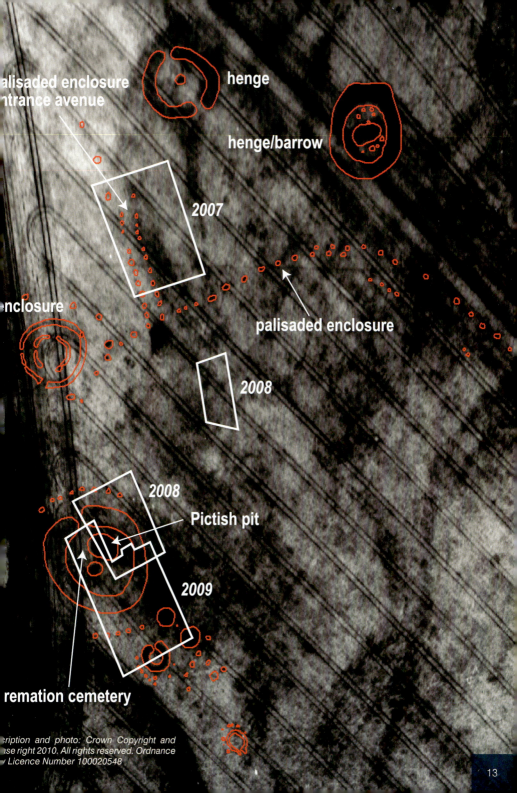

A Neolithic Arena: Palisaded Enclosure

More than 200 pits, which would have supported upright timbers, define the large arena at Forteviot, also referred to as a palisaded enclosure. Roughly circular in shape, this monument encloses an area over 250m in diameter with a narrow entrance avenue on the north side. Comparisons can be drawn with other excavated examples in southern Scotland, but still very little is known about these enigmatic monuments. Dating to within the Later Neolithic (c. 2700 BC) these palisaded enclosures are amongst the largest monuments ever constructed in prehistoric Europe. In 2007 a portion of the avenue to the enclosure was excavated.

Construction and Chronology

Prior to the construction of the avenue and large palisaded enclosure it is believed that this area was wooded because of the presence of several crescent-shaped pits, probably created when living trees fell over or were deliberately pulled over. Two of the tree pits were cut by avenue postholes which, the presence of charcoal suggests, may have been purposefully cleared before the construction of the monument.

All of the avenue postholes which were investigated held massive oak timbers – posts or whole tree trunks – up to 1m in diameter. Judging from the depth of the postholes such timbers could have stood as much as 3 or 4m high, creating an impressive entrance into the enclosure. The avenue, less than 4m in width, would have provided a confined passage which opened out into the awe-inspiring expanse of the enclosure itself. Within the enclosure, great numbers of people could have gathered to participate in ceremonies.

View of the excavations of the massive timber avenue from the air

Radiocarbon dating is not precise enough to reveal how long it took to build the enclosure, but variation in the layout of the postholes seen on the aerial photographs suggest that it was built over many years. Dragging hundreds of large oak logs to this location would in itself have been a time-consuming and labour-intensive activity, in addition to digging postholes without metal tools and erecting the posts.

As time passed, the monument seems to have been transformed: in some cases, posts were removed, while others were burnt where they stood and still others left to rot.

The location of the monumental timber enclosure appears to have remained visible long after the posts disappeared, perhaps marked by hollows where posts had stood. A pit containing burnt material from the medieval period was found within the avenue, and the old road to Forteviot (now a modern field boundary) appears to respect the eastern side of the enclosure.

Reconstruction drawing of the Late Neolithic timber enclosure by Alice Watterson

Cremation Cemetery, Timber Circle and Henge Monument

Excavations of the largest henge at Forteviot in 2008 and 2009 have demonstrated the location to be a focus of activity and ritual over many centuries in prehistory and again, several millennia later, in the Pictish period. During the Later Neolithic, a henge – a space for ritual gatherings defined by a large ditch and earthen bank – was created, replacing an earlier timber circle and encompassing part of an earlier cremation cemetery. The henge monument remained a focus for activity for many centuries and over time its meaning was defined. In the Bronze Age, the henge was adapted when a large cairn covering a megalithic cist burial was inserted into the ditch. Excavation of this undisturbed burial revealed a richly-furnished grave from the Early Bronze Age. Although there are a few traces of later prehistoric presence in the area, it is only in the Pictish period that the monument is clearly redefined, with a large pit cut in the centre of the henge. While the precise nature of this and later activity on the site is still to be resolved, what is clear is that this monument in Forteviot was a powerful magnet for activity over millennia, making it one of the most long-lived ceremonial centres in Scotland.

Cremation Cemetery

At the start of the Later Neolithic period, either before or at the same time that the great timber enclosure was constructed, Forteviot was the site of a cremation cemetery. The excavations uncovered eight discrete burials alongside spreads of later disturbed cremations. The discrete bundles of cremated bone were placed in pits, some buried in organic bags or wooden vessels. Cremation cemeteries of Neolithic date are incredibly rare in Scotland, and its closest parallel of a similar date is a large cremation cemetery found within Stonehenge. Due to later activities on the site, it is not clear if there was a monument, such as a mound or enclosure, marking this cemetery. Nonetheless, it can be suggested that the careful placement of burials may have been one of the reasons why the great timber enclosure, or arena, was built here. After a few centuries, this cemetery became the focus for new activity when a circle of timbers was erected around it, followed by the construction of a henge monument.

The Timber Circle

In the end of the Late Neolithic (c. 2700 BC), a timber circle measuring over 40m in diameter was built of massive oak posts. Over time the posts were either removed or allowed to decay. It was when the timber circle fell out of use, around 2500 BC, that a massive earthwork monument, a henge, was built following the footprint of the timber circle. The ditch of the henge was substantial, up to 3m in depth and 9m wide. The soil cast up from the ditch would have been mounded on the outside creating a relatively small enclosed internal space, only 20m in diameter. This bank may have subsumed any remnants of the timber circle.

Excavators posing in the postholes of the timber circle

The Henge

The construction of the henge at Forteviot was monumental and marked the location that was likely to have been used for ceremonial activity. Debris from feasting and ritual deposition has been found at other sites of this type, and small burnt deposits and some smashed pottery in the ditch hint at such activities at Forteviot.

One of the more peculiar elements of the cropmark complex at Forteviot, located to the south of the henge, is a very small 'henge monument', only 8m in diameter with a ditch 2.5m wide. The elements that compose this monument mirror the larger henge, right down to having a single entrance on the north-west side and a timber circle. The function of this monument and its relationship to the large henge is unknown.

The ditch of the large henge gradually filled in naturally, punctuated only by occasional deposits of burnt turves thrown into the ditch from the interior. However, by the Early Bronze Age, when the ditch was largely backfilled, the character of the activities at this monument had drastically changed. At this time, a high-status dagger burial within a cist was inserted into the henge ditch. The cist and its discovery are discussed separately below.

Pictish Pit in the Centre of the Henge

A large pit within the centre of the henge, dug in the Pictish period (around AD 600), attests to the lasting visibility and significance of the site at least two millennia after it was first built.

This enigmatic pit was roughly circular in plan and over 10m in diameter, with a maximum depth of 1.5m. The sides of the pit slope gently at the top before plunging steeply towards a narrow base containing occasional burnt deposits. In the upper fill of this pit were fragments of iron and lead, Roman amphora fragments and sherds of medieval pottery, suggesting that the feature was deliberately backfilled in the medieval period (around AD 1200). Although the function of this pit is unclear, its location within the henge is unlikely to be a coincidence; the henge (and cairn) would have been visible as low mounds for millennia. Thousands of years after it was first built, the henge was clearly still a focus of activity. Along with the large central pit, the henge ditch was levelled up at a later date by a thick layer of rubble. Objects within this rubble layer include prehistoric worked lithics, a glass droplet and metal objects which probably date from a much later use of the site.

The use, and reuse, of sacred places was not uncommon, but the sequence of events at this monument suggests that it is one of the more complex henge sites known in Scotland.

East-facing section of henge ditch

2cm Sherds of Early Bronze Age Beaker pottery found in the henge ditch; Excavators hard at work on site

Forteviot Cist and Dagger Burial

In August 2009, nearly 4000 years after it had been sealed, an extraordinary Bronze Age cist was opened. The capstone was lifted to reveal material which survived in a remarkable state of preservation. Within the cist were the remains of a dagger and a knife, fragments of wooden vessels, animal hide and, most astonishingly, flowers.

The capstone of the cist was first discovered in 2008, but as it could not be lifted it was reburied. In 2009 a crane was used to lift the stone exposing the cist. Initial inspection of the contents revealed the presence of copper alloy and organic materials, so excavation was undertaken with the support of a specialist conservator (Pieta Greaves, AOC Archaeology Group). Following careful recording, the contents were lifted in blocks so that they could be excavated in a controlled environment.

The Cist Construction

Judging from the type of artefacts it contained, the cist was built around 2100 - 1950 BC, some 500 years after the henge was constructed. Placed within a large pit, the cist was built of big sandstone slabs positioned to make a rough rectangular box (1.7m NE-SW by 1.15m) supported by packing stones, clay and gravel. Specially selected water-worn pebbles formed the floor of the cist. Large quartz pebbles seemed to have been positioned in the south-west end. A layer or mat of birch bark was then laid on the floor of the cist. Onto the bark, grave goods and the body were placed, with the deceased most likely laid in a crouched position lying on his or her side. Although bones have not survived, there appear to be traces of re-mineralised bone adhering to the sides of the cist. Accompanying the body was a rich collection of grave goods, including a bronze dagger and knife, two wooden containers and other organic and stone objects.

Immediately following the burial the cist and its contents were sealed by a huge sandstone slab weighing some 4 tons. This stone must have been skilfully transported, possibly from an outcrop several miles to the north of the site on the other side of the River Earn. Examination of the underside of the capstone revealed an enigmatic carving, which could be described as a stylised axe or club with a spiral or 'eye-shaped' tail. After the cist was sealed it was covered by a cairn of smaller stones.

Clockwise from top: Lifting the capstone of the cist; The enigmatic carving on the underside of the capstone; The bronze dagger surrounded by organic material as it was carefully removed from site; A view of the cist and its contents

The Contents of the Cist and Post-Excavation Analysis

In the months following the excavation, the fragile contents of the cist were conserved and examined by a team of specialists from across the UK. At this stage the findings are provisional, but the range of objects accompanying this special Bronze Age burial is becoming clear.

The combination and variety of the grave goods, the location within a large henge, as well as the rock-art on the capstone are all indications that the individual buried within this cist was socially, politically or ideologically significant to the Bronze Age community of Forteviot.

Other dagger burials have been discovered in Scotland – 42 Bronze Age daggers have previously been recorded. However, the Forteviot cist is one of particular importance because it was excavated under controlled conditions, allowing the suite of organic grave goods to be recovered and for its position within the henge sequence to be appreciated.

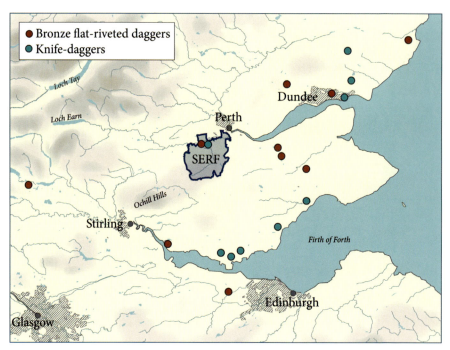

Map of the distribution of Bronze Age daggers in Scotland (after Neil Wilkin)

Organic Offerings

Due to peculiar atmospheric and chemical conditions within the cist, there has been some remarkable organic preservation. Although no human bones or teeth remained intact, fragments of two wooden vessels were present alongside a discrete deposit of plant remains lying under a layer of animal hide (perhaps forming one side of a bag). Initial analysis of the plant material indicates that it was composed largely of meadowsweet flowers (Filipendula ulmaria) – the first conclusive discovery of flowers within a Bronze Age burial in Britain.

The Dagger

The most spectacular artefact is a dagger crafted from a variety of materials. It has been identified as a Butterwick type, dating to between 2100 BC and 1950 BC. The blade is composed of copper alloy, and a ribbed gold band curves around the hilt, which appears to have been made of wood or horn. The pommel, held together by fine wooden pins, may have been made of antler. Traces of a sheath composed of animal skin were identified adhering to the dagger blade.

0   4cm

Forteviot Fire Starter?

Found with the flowers was a distinct collection of items: a piece of limonite – or a similar iron ore – and a worked flint. These materials may have been part of a fire-starting kit. Birch bark, found within the cist, could have been another component of such a kit.

Pictish Forteviot

Documentary sources have highlighted Forteviot as a major Pictish royal centre from at least the mid 9th century AD. Archaeologically, the collection of sculptured crosses within the area of Forteviot, including the unique Forteviot carved stone arch, all point to the presence here of a significant Pictish centre going back into the 8th century. The discovery and excavation of this centre will be important as it would be the first open, undefended royal site which we know of in Scotland, marking a change in practice from the previous hill-top forts such as Dunadd, Dunollie and Edinburgh. Between 2006 and 2008, investigations have been carried out in and around the village of Forteviot looking for traces of this early centre as well as recording the development of the village throughout the medieval period.

Illustration of The Dupplin Cross by Ian G. Scott.

Searching for the Pictish Palace

Preliminary geophysical surveys within Forteviot village were undertaken in 2006 and 2007. The main results of these investigations highlighted traces of an earlier post-medieval town plan in the centre of the village and several other possible structures in the north-east corner of the village and near the Manse. An extensive area was surveyed at Haly Hill – traditionally thought to have been the site of the palace. Although this survey revealed no significant archaeological features, the results had been significantly affected by recent agricultural practices.

Test pits were dug around the village in 2007 and 2008 as a complementary method to the geophysical survey. These pits, predominantly of a standard 1m square, were designed to locate any surviving medieval deposits and to quantify pottery distributions in order to gain some idea of the extent and date of the medieval village.

Results from test pits within the vicinity of Haly Hill confirmed Leslie Alcock's findings from the 1980s that no trace remained of any medieval deposits, either on the hill, or below in the alluvial floodplain. Study of the 18th-century accounts of the palace being washed away suggests these may be confusing the palace with later medieval buildings, and that the palace site lay elsewhere, possibly under the present manse or further south.

The test pits in gardens on the north side of the village did produce medieval pottery, including Scottish White Gritty Ware of 12th/13th-century date, as well as green-glazed wares of later medieval date. However, all this material came from a buried medieval ploughsoil, indicating that the core of the medieval village lay closer to the present street line. In 2008 several more pits were excavated to the south of the village, which produced little sign of medieval stratigraphy. These areas were mostly far from the village street. Although further areas remain to be investigated, the results so far have given us a good idea of the limits of the medieval village, which is very similar to the present one, and has given us an indication of where the early deposits might survive.

A plaque noting the death of Kenneth mac Alpin at Forteviot

Forteviot Church

Study of the parish church has shown it to be on the site of a medieval predecessor, and so possibly the site of an early monastery, but no sign of Pictish occupation has so far been identified. Stumps of two walls and a possible buttress projecting from the east wall show that the rebuilding of the church in 1778 incorporated parts of an earlier building, which was probably the medieval church documented since the 13th century. The topography of the churchyard has also been investigated, showing a low mound to the south of the present building and a series of post-medieval tombstones dating to as early as 1690. All this suggests that the putative Pictish church may have been in roughly the same location as the present church, and confirms a high-status focus on the south side of the village. Stray finds collected within the manse grounds include an 18th century sundial, an Iron Age quern, a date-stone of 1686 (possibly from the earlier manse) and a possible medieval quern.

Forteviot parish church and churchyard

Pictish Cemetery

The Pictish cemetery at Forteviot, identified from aerial photographs, is one of the largest known in Scotland. Two areas within the cemetery were excavated in 2007 and 2009, targeting different forms of burial monuments including square and round barrows as well as unenclosed graves. Part of a large square enclosure, situated in the north-east corner of the cemetery was also investigated, revealing evidence which suggest it may have been the site of a Romano-Celtic temple. Potentially earlier than the cemetery, this enclosure may have retained its cult significance in the Pictish period, as it appears to have been respected by the surrounding burials. The whole cemetery seems to have been given over to agricultural use around the 13th century, when its significance was forgotten or perhaps deliberately destroyed.

Square Enclosure

Towards the north end of the Pictish cemetery is a large square enclosure, measuring roughly 30m square overall. It was the aim of this excavation to shed light on the possible function of this enclosure which lay so close to and was partly surrounded by the cemetery. In 2009, excavation of the north-east area of this enclosure showed that the ditch was approximately 2m in width with a steep V-shaped profile. The contents of the ditch were particularly clean, lacking in any domestic debris or artefacts, making dating difficult, but showing that it was not a domestic settlement. Within the interior of the enclosure was a scatter of eight pits with three distinct characters – small charcoal-filled, small stone-filled and large stone-filled. These pits had no coherent pattern and were unlikely to have formed part of any structures. Only two of these pits could be dated using radiocarbon methods. Surprisingly, one of these was dated to the Late Bronze Age and another to the 14th century. The character of the ditch, the shape of the enclosure, as well as the associated finds in this area, however, suggest that the enclosure may have been a Romano-British religious building of a type well known in southern England but rare in the north. Although perhaps built centuries earlier, this enclosure appears to have been respected as the Pictish cemetery was constructed immediately around it. The Bronze Age date hints at earlier ritual use and suggests that the Pictish cemetery was located in an area of long-standing ritual activity.

Right: Aerial view of the excavation of the Pictish cemetery in 2009

Barrows and Unenclosed Graves

The cemetery consists of both square and round barrows as well as unenclosed burials arranged both in rows and more randomly. Barrows are monumental burials, with a large central earthen mound placed over the grave and a surrounding ditch. Unlike the simple dug graves, the barrows would have been very conspicuous – and appear to have been constructed for a select few. At Forteviot, the cemetery has been truncated by agricultural practices, such as rig and furrow cultivation and modern ploughing, over many centuries. Nonetheless, under the topsoil the dug features of the cemetery were still visible. The soil conditions, however, do not support the preservation of bone and therefore few human remains were identified during excavation.

Excavations in 2007 explored two conjoined square barrows dating to the 8th/9th centuries AD. The barrows measured approximately 8m square, with causeways across the ditches at each corner. Although the orientation and character of both barrows mirrored one another, there were several irregularities, suggesting that one was built later than the other. Within each of the barrows, the central grave was aligned east to west and surrounded by an unusual four 'post' setting. Only the very outer enamel of teeth of the interred body survived and no associated grave goods were found.

Several unenclosed graves – both small, so presumably child graves, and larger adult graves – were also uncovered. All of them appeared to respect the barrows and were aligned east to west. Two of these graves contained fragments of outer teeth enamel, surviving in the west end of the graves. A date from one of these graves was from the 9th/10th centuries AD suggesting it may be contemporary with or slightly later than the barrows.

In 2009 a round barrow was excavated. The central grave was also aligned east to west but no human remains were found here. When the grave was partly filled, two burnt wooden artefacts were deposited and may suggest a particular burial rite associated with this barrow. The grave dated to the 4th/5th centuries AD.

On either side of the round barrow were two unenclosed graves. One of the graves, located to the east of the round barrow, yielded the remains of a charred oak log coffin, which is unique at Forteviot so far and was dated roughly to the same period as the round barrow grave, i.e. the 4th/6th centuries AD. These dates show the cemetery had a long life, starting well before the documented royal use of the site in the 9th century.

Clockwise from top left: The remains of teeth found in the Pictish cemetery; Excavation of the round barrow; Aerial photograph with the cropmarks of the Pictish cemetery outlined in red; Unenclosed graves excavated in 2007

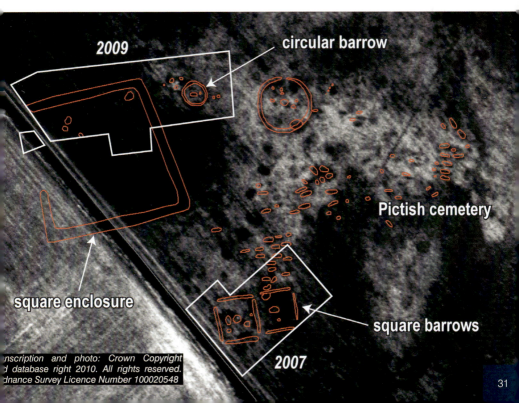

Forts around Forteviot

The remains of ancient forts are situated in prominent positions in the hills surrounding Forteviot. Many of these stand on the northern slopes of the Ochils, with extensive views across Strathearn. Forts would have held a variety of roles for the local communities, but were thought to have predominantly been conspicuous centres of power of the later prehistoric and early medieval periods. There are at least ten forts or large defended settlement sites near Forteviot that we hope to explore. The results of small-scale excavations will provide a rare and much needed regional sequence for hillforts and will outline their development in the Strathearn landscape. So far three sites have been excavated as part of this study: Jackschairs Wood, Dunknock and Green of Invermay.

Castle Law, Forgandenny hillfort in the snow

Jackschairs Wood

In 2007 Jackschairs Wood was the first hillfort to be excavated by SERF. This site was often thought, first by antiquarians in the 19th century, to have been the precursor to the palace at Forteviot, situated only a few miles to the south-east of the village. Jackschairs Wood fort is defined by four ramparts and at least three ditches, all of which follow the contours of the hilltop and enclose an internal area that is dominated by a substantial central rock outcrop. Although relatively lowlying, there would have been extensive views to the north-east and west.

A 35m by 1.5m trench was excavated across the ditches and ramparts and into the interior of the hillfort. The excavations revealed a number of features.

Within the interior of the fort the preservation was variable; nonetheless, under layers which represent destruction of the fort's defences there were traces of an internal corridor and stone paving. Excavation of the ramparts and ditches revealed the innermost rampart to have an inner stone facing of which three courses survived and which incorporated a large upright boulder, which would have supported an equally substantial timber post. Evidence for the subsequent destruction of the timber was preserved in the primary charcoal-rich layers of the innermost ditch. By comparison, the outer three ditches contained relatively 'clean' fills and were less complex. The outer ramparts were simply made of earth and lacked signs of additional structural features.

A series of radiocarbon dates places the construction and use of all three ditches, as well as the features within the interior, to the Early Iron Age (700-400 BC). This suggests that Jackschairs was constructed and used within a relatively short space of time. There is at present no evidence to suggest that the hillfort at Jackschairs was an immediate predecessor to a Pictish palace at Forteviot.

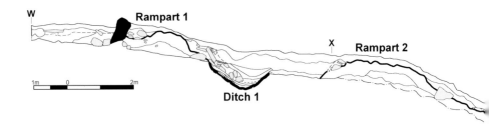

Clockwise from top: The interior of the fort under excavation; View of the ramparts downslope; Line drawing of the ramparts and ditches of Jackschairs; View of the ramparts towards the interior

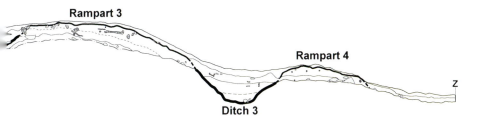

Dunknock

Dunknock is a low but conspicuous hill overlooking the village of Dunning. Over the years, a wide range of objects dating from the Neolithic to the medieval period, including a Bronze Age socketed axehead, have been found on Dunknock, which attests to the significance of this place over millennia. The fort was first identified through cropmarks and consists of at least four roughly parallel ditches that curve around the contour of the hill.

The fort was examined through small-scale excavations in 2008 and 2009. The earliest dated feature was a narrow Late Bronze Age (around 1200-1000 BC) ditch located on the east side of the hill. However, most of the evidence recorded appears to derive from a substantial Early Iron Age (700-400 BC) settlement. During the Early Iron Age, Dunknock became a focus of intense settlement and activity. The hill was significantly modified through the construction of several massive ditches and ramparts. However, it seems that the fort, in this monumental form, did not last long.

On the west side of the hill, excavations in 2008 revealed evidence of one of the collapsed ramparts of the fort, and in 2009, in conjunction with SERF, Glasgow Archaeological Research Division (GUARD) returned to this feature and extended the excavations further downslope. The results showed that the rampart was largely made of earth and had been reinforced with timber and stone. The rampart was built on a levelled pebble surface and a temporary timber palisade was erected to help with its construction. Some time later, the rampart was destroyed, the timbers were burnt and the rampart collapsed downslope. A portion of a ditch was uncovered, which produced a notable amount of later prehistoric pottery.

GUARD excavating at Dunknock

On the east side of the hill, just above the crest of the slope, traces of a possible rectangular scooped structure were uncovered. Sherds of coarse prehistoric pottery, daub – the outer coating for a wattle wall – as well as fragments of both saddle and rotary querns were found within this structure. Radiocarbon dates suggest that this structure was in use when Dunknock was a fort. Nearer to the summit of the hill, a substantial pit or dug-feature with a complex series of deposits – also dating to the Early Iron Age – was discovered.

Further west, around the contour of hill, another trench was excavated but no clear traces of the fort were found. It is possible that the ditches and rampart were not continuous, but were only built on the north – and most visible – side of Dunknock. This hillfort would have been an impressive visual monument. During the Roman Iron Age, several centuries later, a large temporary camp – some of which is still visible in Kincladie Wood – was built in the shadow of Dunknock, along a supposed prehistoric routeway.

Subsequent activities at Dunknock may have been temporary. However, later cultivation of the summit of the hill has greatly disturbed or completely removed any less substantial traces of the past.

The multiple ditches of the fort at Dunknock visible as cropmarks from the air

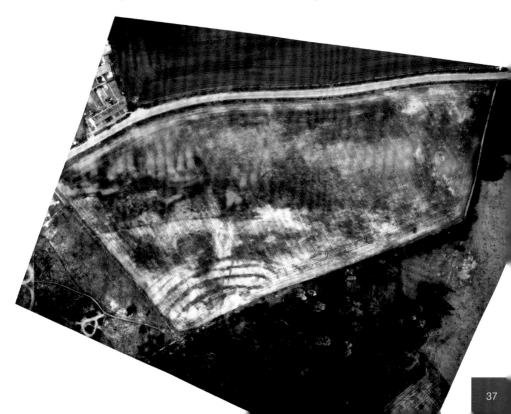

Green of Invermay Enclosure and Doocot

A substantial enclosure at the Green of Invermay is located on the edge of a steep river terrace. Lying less than 1.5km to the south of Forteviot, this enclosure is only visible as cropmarks from the air. Although not a hillfort, its substantial ditch and location suggests that this enclosure was an important prehistoric defended settlement. However, the excavations in 2009 indicate the site was likely to be a 12th to 14th century medieval earthwork or moated site. At a later date, a doocot was constructed at its north-eastern end. The doocot may have marked the location of the ancient centre as the core of the estate moved upstream in the 16th century.

The Enclosure

In 2009 a trench was excavated through the interior of the enclosure and into the ditch. The ditch was over 1.2m deep and the initial fills suggest that it had been rapidly backfilled. Subsequent shallow deposits consisted of ash and rubble with 12th to 14th century pottery. The uppermost fills of the ditch also contained medieval pottery – Scottish White Gritty Ware – which were being swept or dumped into the ditch from the interior of the enclosure.

A palisade slot was discovered some 9m inside the ditch, which would have supported a continuous line of timbers, reinforced and packed with stones. The palisade may have been an internal division within the enclosure.

The interior had been severely disturbed by centuries of cultivation. Nonetheless, there were scant traces of medieval occupation with associated pottery and metalwork. Within the plough soil, a trumpet-headed brooch from the 1st to 2nd century AD was found. This single artefact suggests that there may have been earlier activity on this site. The lack of post-medieval finds from this site, even from the upper plough layers, suggests that by the 18th century the area was no longer a focus of settlement at this time, but instead became an open field within the reorganised estate.

The enclosure at the Green of Invermay is tentatively interpreted as being the original baronial centre of the Innermeath Estate. Pont's map of the late 16th century shows that the focus of the estate had shifted by this time further upstream along the Water of May, near the present day estate house.

Fragments of the Roman Iron Age brooch found at the Green of Invermay

Above: Excavation at the enclosure at the Green of Invermay; Below: The broad curved ditch of the Green of Invermay enclosure seen from the air

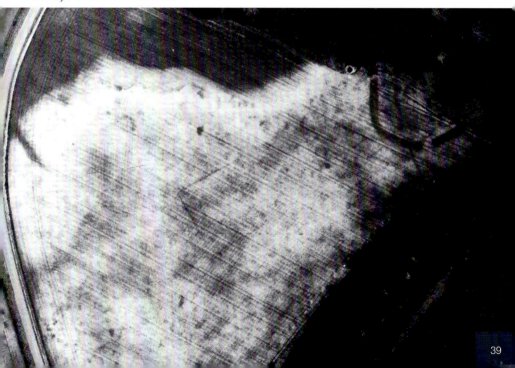

The Doocot

The doocot takes the form of a tall (6.5m) and narrow (4.0m) tower with little ornamental detail apart from the small tooth-shaped fixtures crowning the wallhead and a very slight plinth course. The tower is constructed of several varieties of local sandstones, some of which are distinct. Originally the building was harled (lime-coated), but only a few traces of render remain and these are confined to northern sides and the lower levels. The door is located on the south-west elevation, and above it a rectangular opening had been inserted and subsequently enlarged. This opening provided an access for the pigeons; grooves in the frame indicate the presence of further small openings. Presumably, the original bird entrance was via a cupola in the roof. The building is in good condition (about 80% of the pigeon boxes remain) and weather-tight thanks to a new roof.

The location of the doocot is atypical in that it is not convenient for Invermay House or the lodge house. It is prominently positioned on the crest of a steep scarp on the west side of the Water of May, where it would have been a conspicuous feature from the old Bridge of Earn-Dunning road which formerly passed through the centre of Invermay estate (Innermeath). It may be that the doocot was located here to mark the ancient estate centre when the centre was shifted 1km upstream, to Old Invermay House. Old Invermay House is a complex structure, which was probably built in the late 16th century and later extended in 1633. Amongst the building material used in the core of Old Invermay House are blocks of distinctive sandstone, as seen in the doocot, suggesting that the doocot is contemporary with Old Invermay House.

The south-east facing elevation of the doocot at the Green of Invermay; background image: an excerpt from the OS First Edition 1:10,560 scale map, 1862

Early Chapels

SERF has begun to explore the less well-known remains of the early chapels at Exmagirdle and Muckersie. In due course it is planned to examine all the medieval churches within the study area. This earliest phase of Christianity is not well documented on mainland Scotland and chapels like Exmagirdle and Muckersie may well provide a key to understanding this transitional period. The early development of the Church in Scotland also went hand in hand with political development and power networks, and therefore these sites are significant in the wider evolution of the area in the medieval period.

The early medieval tower of St. Serf's church, Dunning

Exmagirdle

Exmagirdle, or Ecclesmagirdle, church is a ruined single-celled building occupying a small, curvilinear churchyard within the Glenearn Estate. The name of Exmagirdle derives from ecclesia (Latin for 'church') and is dedicated to St Grillán, a companion of St Columba. Both the usage of 'ecclesia' and the dedication suggests an early ecclesiastical foundation for this chapel, perhaps going back to the 7th or 8th century. In linguistic terms, Exmagirdle is the oldest church in the study area and it is also one of the best documented, having been the object of a dispute between Dunblane Cathedral and Lindores Abbey. It survived as a place of worship until the 18th century although it was incorporated into Dron parish in 1652.

In 2007 fieldwork here included a measured survey of the church, a topographic survey of the churchyard, documentation of the burial monuments and a geophysical survey of the open areas around the kirkyard. The small, single-celled church retains some medieval architectural features, including the east window and an aumbry of 15th-century date or earlier. Although the church has been substantially rebuilt, its proportions – 9.5m by 5.5m – and its setting suggest that it is substantially medieval. Although few in number, there is a fascinating collection of 40 post-medieval burial monuments within the kirkyard providing a unique insight into the composition of rural community of the 17th and 18th centuries and, from the mid 19th century, the lairds of Gleanearn. These monuments range from elaborate recumbent slabs of the local freeholders to a series of fine headstones erected by farmers and tradesmen, a number of crude stone markers and the finely carved plaques of the modern landowners. Andrew Gourlay was able to identify the majority of those commemorated in local parish records for his MA dissertation (2009).

On the south and east sides of the curving kirkyard the boundary appears to follow an ancient line, although the wall itself has been heavily rebuilt. To the north and west the churchyard had been truncated in post-medieval times to accommodate developments in the farm layout.

Geophysical survey outside the north of the church attempted to locate the original line of the kirkyard, but this was unproductive, probably because of the extent of the landscaping in this area. Within the gardens around the laird's house, geophysical survey was more successful. It was possible to define the line of the barmkin wall which once enclosed Exmagirdle House, built in 1548, and included a mock-turret doocot in its circuit as well as monumental gateway, both of which are still intact.

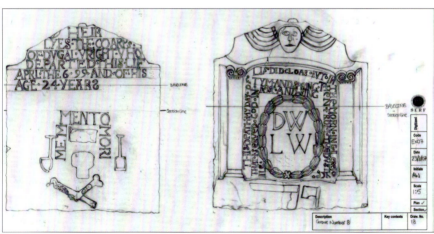

Top: Recording a gravestone in Exmagirdle churchyard. Bottom: Field drawing of above gravestone

Muckersie

Muckersie chapel is a ruined single-celled building situated in a small, oval churchyard within the Invermay Estate on the southern perimeter of its policies. The medieval dedication at Muckersie has been lost, but the earliest certain reference indicates that the church served as an independent parsonage of the estates of Bishops of Dunkeld. After the Reformation it continued to be a place of worship until 1638 when it was amalgamated with Forteviot parish. Subsequently, the ruined church was restored as a chapel and mausoleum by the Lord of Invermay.

A standing building survey of the chapel and a topographic survey of the churchyard were carried out in 2008. The chapel is built of local sandstone and stands to gable height, although all the walls have been substantially modified in post-medieval times.

Three broad phases of use can be identified. The earliest masonry is coursed rubble which survived in the lower portions of the eastern wall and the lower south-western corner of the western wall. Although there were no datable features *in situ*, it seems likely that this represents the extent of the medieval parish church. The second phase relates to the post-Reformation refurbishment of the parish. Along with the additions, such as the crow-stepped gable, at this time the south wall was rebuilt and a central door with two flanking windows inserted.

The final phase of refurbishment involved the extensive reworking of the ruinous building, which included the construction of a massive new doorway in a pointed arch in the western elevation and blocking the openings in the south wall. This phase of refurbishment was undertaken in the mid 19th century to provide a mausoleum and chapel for the Invermay Estate. The late medieval octagonal font from Muckersie was given to Forteviot church in 1905.

Right: Standing building survey of the interior of Muckersie chapel; background image: East-facing elevation drawing of Muckersie chapel

Dunning

In 2009 a 3-D digital scan was made of the exterior of St Serf's in Dunning by Historic Scotland Technical Conservation Group and Glasgow School of Art's Digital Design Studio. This survey will provide the basis for a new analysis of the fabric, which will allow the features of this remarkable building to be better understood. Perhaps the most significant insights relate to the prominent sockets visible on all the faces of the tower. Consideration of their position and form indicates that they most likely supported timber balconies, which presumably had a liturgical function. The new digital survey provides an excellent platform to explore various possible reconstructions.

Data from the 3D laser scan of the early medieval tower at St. Serf's church

Upland Survey

With the aim of exploring the wider landscape of Forteviot – and the ever-changing relationship between people and land – the survey of the upland zone to the south of Dunning and Forteviot provides an opportunity to document the development of agriculture and settlement, particularly before and after the period of Improvement in the 18th and early 19th centuries. It is also a chance to explore communication and transportation routes across Strathearn and the Ochils, some of which may have prehistoric origins. Between 2007 and 2009, small teams have systematically walked four areas recording any archaeological features.

Walkover survey in the uplands of Strathearn

Prehistory

Only a few traces of prehistoric activity have so far been recorded. The Gray Stone, a prehistoric standing stone 2.13m high with a roughly triangular plan, lies to the south of Knowes Farm. Over time this monument has been reinterpreted; according to local stories, perhaps of some antiquity, the Gray Stone is said to have been the gravestone of, or memorial to, the Mormaer of Atholl, who died at the Battle of Duncrub in AD 965.

There are also hints of a largely invisible later prehistoric settlement in this landscape. Two previously unrecorded hut platforms, one on the north-east facing slopes of Mount Eldritch, and the other on the Cleavage Hills have been found.

Pre-Improvement Cultivation

A striking aspect of the archaeology of this landscape has been the complexes of turf enclosures and dykes, as seen on Boghall and Casken hills. Some of the dykes are remarkably substantial, such as one recorded east of Knock of Boghall which measured 1.5m wide and 0.5m high. The complexity and sheer number of enclosures in the uplands suggest that they were constructed for the 18th-century practice of 'tathing', where livestock were grazed in specific enclosures which would be cultivated the next year, thus ensuring they were properly manured.

Associated with these turf enclosures were areas of rig and furrow cultivation. Some were well-preserved and characterised by broad rigs, an early form of cultivation that was still in use in the mid 18th century. Others areas were defined by narrower rig – a product of splitting wide rigs by adding another furrow in between – and were likely to have been the main form of cultivation in the period immediately before Improvement in the mid 18th century. The identification of different types of cultivation, as well as short-lived extensions of cultivation beyond the head-dyke, attests to the varied history of agriculture on these slopes. Crops of oats, with some bere barley and legumes, were thought to have been grown in this environment, but by the late 18th century very little of the uplands were cultivated.

Also found in relation to the turf dyke complexes, were small, apparently turf-built structures, normally found isolated or in pairs, with typical and consistent dimensions of 8–9m x 5–6m. These structures are clearly larger and more elaborate than shielings, and do not show the expected clustering of shielings. It is tempting to see this apparent dispersed settlement pattern as a precursor of the familiar nucleated post-Medieval settlements. However, both at Casken Hill and Boghall they are often associated with broad rig and furrow, which is probably as late as 17th or 18th century.

Top: A student stands next to a Bronze Age hut platform found on Eldritch Hill; bottom: Investigating a possible archaeological feature on the Black Hill of Kippen

Farmsteads

About 1km to the south-east of Knowes Farm, is the medieval farmstead of Blaeberry Hill. Blaeberry Hill is the modern name of an abandoned settlement, possibly the one depicted as Blackberryhill on Stobie's map of 1783, and may have been documented as early as 1565. The survey revealed traces of this farmstead within a forestry enclave. This is a complex farmstead. The clearest structure at the date of visit had a range of five roughly square rooms, each measuring about 5 x 5m, with another rubble structure built over the two northerly rooms. The most striking feature of this settlement was a substantial perimeter V-shaped ditch with low flanking earthen dykes. There is a possible entrance on the northern side. This feature is strongly reminiscent of enclosures for settlement and cultivation within medieval royal or baronial hunting forests.

The ruins of more recent farmsteads were also recorded. Some of these are located at the site of modern farms, but others such as Rashie Lees, where there are notable remains, are earlier predecessors.

Stone dykes and quarries

Largely thought to be later than the turf dykes, and therefore dating to the post-Improvement period, stone dykes were used to reinforce land divisions and create new enclosures in the uplands. On Casken Hill, turf enclosures were clearly seen to underlie stone dykes and therefore predate the Improvement-period boundaries. In some cases, the stone used to construct these dykes was quarried right next to the boundary. Along the length of the stone dyke between Keltie Estate and Knowes Farm several quarries were recorded.

Route from Common of Dunning to Dunning Village

On the last day of the 2009 survey season, a non-systematic walk was undertaken between the Common of Dunning and the village of Dunning. The aim of this walk was to look for evidence of the historic transhumance route between Dunning and its common grazings – perhaps of medieval origin. This walk highlighted the natural topographic features which define the route and how both humans and cattle have made their mark. On the summit of Chapel Hill, which marks a topographical boundary with the Common, is a substantial turf dyke defining the boundary between the Common and the land to the north. To the east, a sharply-defined cleft between Chapel Hill and North Hill may have formed a natural 'entrance' to the Common from the north, with traffic channelled towards this point by the substantial dyke.

Moving north from Chapel Hill, passing over Priest's Knowe and Eldritch Hill in the direction of Knowes Farm, several discrete sections of braided trackways were identified, appearing as deeply eroded grooves on the steeps slopes and petering out on the level ground. These trackways were created as livestock dug in while climbing upslope, and were accentuated by water erosion. The most extensive section of braided trackway comprised up to 12 individual tracks, some of which had been eroded to a depth of *c*.2m.

Natural places and visibility: the Grey Mare

A natural boulder depicted as 'The Grey Mare' on maps as far back as 1866, but known to locals as 'The Mare and Foal' because of a smaller stone immediately to its south-east, is situated on the north-west slopes of Boghall Hill. Unless obscured by vegetation, it would have been a highly visible landmark to viewers at Boghall Farm, or to travellers along a putative Medieval route following the base of the Ochils. Conspicuous stones such as this commonly had a range of associations, such as acting as a boundary marker in a land charter, marking a place for paying rent or holding a fair, or showing to those in the know where illicit whisky was distilled.

Recording the Grey Mare

SERF: Research in Progress

The aims of the SERF project are fundamental to the understanding of the origins of Scotland and, by design, this is a long-term pursuit. It will take time to fully appreciate what Forteviot can tell us about the ritual practices and burial rites of the earliest farming communities in northern Britain or how the Picts sought to connect their religious and political activaties with those of their Neolithic ancestors. Similarly, we are just beginning to get a grasp on how the agricultural regimes and settlement systems evolved in Strathearn. Further seasons of fieldwork accompanied by scientific analysis are required to properly investigate the exceptionally rich group of hillforts, cropmarks and upland landscapes found in this part of Perthshire. In future years we plan to continue our programme of sampling hillforts and mapping the relics of farming in the Ochils. We also plan to excavate other cropmark sites to gain a balanced picture of life in Strathearn through the ages.

This extended programme of research is necessary if we are to meet our ambitious objectives, but already we have made discoveries which are reshaping our understanding of the past. Some of these results – such as the radiocarbon dates – are disseminated here for the first time, other results which require more reflection and justification are appearing in academic publications. The SERF project team recognises an obligation to inform a range of audiences about our work. In addition to this interim report we provide a full programme of public lectures across the country and beyond. Although we are only in the field for a few weeks a year, new information about the project is constantly being produced, and you can follow along via the internet:

www.gla.ac.uk/departments/archaeology/research/projects/serf/

www.antiquity.ac.uk/projgall/driscoll323/

The general background and context of the research can be explored in the suggestions for further reading. More detailed information about the SERF project can be found in the scholarly publications listed below. These represent the first stage of publication and as work progresses inevitably more publications will follow, which will be listed on the project website.

Further readings on themes introduced in this booklet:

John Hunter and Ian Ralston (eds) 2010 *The Archaeology of Britain: An Introduction from the Earliest Times to the Twenty-first Century*, 2nd edition, London: Routledge.

Gordon Noble 2006 *Neolithic Scotland: Timber, Stone, Earth and Fire*, Edinburgh University Press.

Sally Foster 2004 *Picts, Gaels and Scots*, London: Batsford.

Stephen T. Driscoll 2002 *Alba: The Gaelic Kingdom of Scotland AD 800–1124*, Edinburgh: Birlinn.

Nick Aitchison 2006 *Forteviot: A Pictish and Scottish Royal Centre*, Stroud: Tempus.

Scholarly works supported by the SERF project:

Gordon Noble and Kenneth Brophy (forthcoming) 'Big Enclosures: The Later Neolithic Palisaded Enclosures of Scotland in their North-western European Context', *European Journal of Archaeology*.

Stephen T. Driscoll and Katherine S. Forsyth 2009 'Symbols of Power in Ireland and Scotland, 8th-10th centuries', in F. J. F. Conde and C. García de Castro Valdés (eds) *Poder y simboloía en Europa Siglos VIII-X*, Oviedo, Spain.

Stephen T. Driscoll 2010 'Pictish Archaeology: Persistent Problems and Structural Solutions', in S. T. Driscoll, J. Geddes and M. A. Hall (eds) *Pictish Progress: New Studies on Northern Britain in the Early Middle Ages*, Leiden: Brill.

Stephen T. Driscoll 2010 'SERFing the Scottish Heartlands' *Scottish Archaeological Journal* 32. Proceedings of the Royal Society of Edinburgh Workshop: Identifying Scotland – Context and Collaboration.

Stephen T. Driscoll (in press) 'Was Forteviot Scotland's Tara?', in C. Newman et al. (eds) *Landscapes of Cult and Kingship*, Dublin: Wordwell.

TIMELINE

	3000 BC	2500 BC	2000 BC	1500 BC
DUNKNOCK HILLFORT				
DUNNING SETTLEMENT				
EXMAGIRDLE CHAPEL				
FORTEVIOT CEMETERY				
FORTEVIOT PREHISTORIC COMPLEX		PALISADED ENCLOSURE CREMATION CEMETERY	TIMBER CIRCLE HENGE	CIST
FORTEVIOT SETTLEMENT				
GREEN OF INVERMAY				
JACKSCHAIRS WOOD HILLFORT				
MUCKERSIE CHAPEL				
	3000 BC	2500 BC	2000 BC	1500 BC

Neolithic — Bronze Age

Adoption of farming and woodland clearance (c. 3800 BC)

Construction of Cleaven Dyke Cursus (c. 3300 BC)

Beaker pottery introduced into Scotland
Introduction of metal-working

| | BC | 500 BC | 0 | 500 AD | 1000 AD | 1500 AD | 2000 AD |

SURE · HILLFORT

ST SERF'S TOWER BUILT (1100)
TOWER REMODELLED (1718)
THANAGE
VILLAGE REBUILT (1790s)
CHAPEL BUILT · CHAPEL REBUILT (1548)
SQUARE ENCLOSURE · UNENCLOSED GRAVES
ROUND BARROW
LOG COFFIN GRAVE
SQUARE BARROW
LARGE PIT IN HENGE

CHURCH
DUPPLIN CROSS
PICTISH SCULPTURE
EARLY VILLAGE
ROMAN IRON AGE BROOCH · ENCLOSURE · DOOCOT
HILLFORT
CHAPEL

| BC | 500 BC | 0 | 500 AD | 1000 AD | 1500 AD | 2000 AD |

Iron Age | Roman Incursions | Pictish Kingdom | Kingdom of Alba | Kingdom of Scotland | United Kingdom

- Hillforts, duns and brochs in Scotland
- ow log boat carved
- Construction of Gask Ridge, Roman Frontier works (70-80 AD)
- Battle of Mons Graupius (83/84 AD)
- St Columba founds Iona (563 AD)
- Death of Kenneth mac Alpin (858 AD)
- MacBeth, King of Scots (1040-57 AD)
- Wars of Scottish Independence (1296-1328 & 1332-1357 AD)
- Scottish Reformation (1650 AD)

Acknowledgements

The hard work that has gone into this project is the result of many people and we would like thank all of those who have contributed to the remarkable discoveries that have been unearthed so far and the continued success of this project.

SERF Project Team
Kenneth Brophy, Ewan Campbell, Chris Dalglish, Stephen T. Driscoll, Nick Evans, Michael Given, Meggen Gondek, Allan Hall, Jeremy Huggett, Lorraine McEwan, Gordon Noble, Gert Peterson, Tessa Poller, Dene Wright

Landowners, Farmers and Factors
Without access to the land we would not have been able to undertake any of this work and we wish to record our sincere thanks to the landowner, farmers and factors of Forteviot and the surrounding areas who have facilitated our work. Particularly, we would like to thank Lord Forteviot, the Dupplin Estate, Peter Grewar and Bill McIntosh for allowing us to excavate and survey in and around Forteviot. We would also like to thank Lady Wemyss and the Invermay Estate, Charles and Fiona Wemyss, Jimmy Colthart, Jim and John Craig, Brian Henderson, Lord Rollo of Pitcairns, Robert McPhail, Callum Rollo and the Keltie Estate, Mr and Mrs Queisser and the Glenearn Estate, Stewart Scott, Ann and David Myles, George Ritchie, Duncan MacCrae, Theresa Edwards, Murray Smith, Rosie Newton, and Perth and Kinross Council. We hope that the results to date justify the inconveniences that our presence has caused and hope we can anticipate continued support in the future.

Staff and Supervisors 2006-2009
Kirsten Bedigan, Tamsin Calder, Liam Clancy, Martin Goldberg, Aoife Gould, Cathy MacIver, John Malcolm, Kirsty Millican, Anne-Marie O'Donnell, Elizabeth Pierce, Daniel Sahlen, Sarah Thomas, Rebecca Younger

Students and Volunteers 2006-2009
Coralie Acheson, Peter Aherne, Alexander Aitchison, Sara Al-Haddad, Doreen Ashton, Ann Aves, Natalia Bain, Jean Baxter, Chris Bowles, Lauren Braid, David Buckley, Lawrence Buckley, Rachael Burrell, Kimberley Butler, Sarah Bryson, Kirsten Campbell, Rowan Campbell, Frazer Capie, Roslyn Chapman, Beichen Chen, Andrew Clark, Ross Clark, Katrina Clippert, Graeme Collie, Tom Craig, Jim Crombie, Carmen Cuenca-Garcia, Vicky Davidson, Marije de Vries, Paul Dickson, Stephen Digney, Christina Donald, Byron Edens, Val Ferguson, Tracey Finnigan, Robert Fyans, Andrew Gallagher, Martin Gibson, Peggy Golk, Kirsty Goodwin, Andrew Gourlay, Dorothy Graves, Kieran Grant, Kenneth Green, Carol Greig, Isabel Hall, Sami Harju, Vivi Harris, Jamie Henderson, Bruce Henry, Candace Howie, Kirk Hunter, Benjamin Inglis-Grant, Clark Innes, Danae Karagiannopoulou, Marylène Ladril, Jack Lyttle, Kenny Macrae, Janet MacDougall, Caroline MacGillivray, Flora Mackinnon-Pryde, Gail Mackintosh, Adrian Maldonado, Ian Marshall, Michael Marshall, Janene May, Morgana McCabe, Richard McClay, Robert McCorrisken, Laura McGeoch, David McGowran, Lachlan McKeggie, Gordon McKellar, Kathleen McKelvie, Camilla McLachlan, Catriona McLeod,